CREATING THANKSGIVING CRAFTS

By Dana Meachen Rau • Illustrated by Kathleen Petelinsek

CHERRY LAKE PUBLISHING • ANN ARBOR, MICHIGAN

CHERRY LAKE Publishing

Published in the United States of America by Cherry Lake Publishing
Ann Arbor, Michigan
www.cherrylakepublishing.com

Content Adviser: Dr. Julia Hovanec, Department of Arts Education and Crafts, Kutztown University of Pennsylvania, Kutztown, Pennsylvania

Photo Credits: Page 4, ©Julija Sapic/Shutterstock, Inc.; page 5, ©Debby Wong/Shutterstock, Inc.; page 6, ©David Monette/Alamy; page 8, ©Bochkarev Photography/Shutterstock, Inc.; page 9, ©Brent Hofacker/Shutterstock, Inc.; pages 18 and 23, ©Dana Meachen Rau; page 29, ©Monkey Business Images/Dreamstime.com.

Library of Congress Cataloging-in-Publication Data
Rau, Dana Meachen, 1971–
   Creating Thanksgiving crafts / by Dana Meachen Rau.
      pages cm. — (How-to library) (Crafts)
   Audience: Grade 4 to 6.
   Includes bibliographical references and index.
   ISBN 978-1-62431-148-2 (library binding) —
ISBN 978-1-62431-280-9 (paperback) —
ISBN 978-1-62431-214-4 (e-book)
   1. Thanksgiving decorations—Juvenile literature.
   2. Handicraft—Juvenile literature. I. Title.

   TT900.T5R38 2013   745.594'1649—dc23
2013013658

Cherry Lake Publishing would like to acknowledge the work of The Partnership for 21st Century Skills. Please visit www.p21.org for more information.

Printed in the United States of America
Corporate Graphics Inc.
July 2013
CLFA13

HOW-TO LIBRARY

TABLE OF CONTENTS

Thanks a Lot!

Think about all of the good things in your life. Maybe you enjoy playing sports. Perhaps you spend your time making crafts, writing stories, or drawing pictures. Do you like talking with your friends, hanging out with your family, or meeting new people? Do you enjoy roller coasters, walking your dog, or eating a yummy ice cream sundae? Take a moment to appreciate the things that make you happy.

You might be thankful for your pet!

There is a day every year set aside for giving thanks—Thanksgiving! Friends and family take a break from work and school to spend time visiting and feasting together. Everyone has different Thanksgiving **traditions**. Some people go to parades or watch them on television. Some families play or watch football. You might sit down to a large meal of turkey with all the trimmings. You might find a way to help others.

No matter how you celebrate, you can make crafts to add fun to the holiday festivities. Your friends and family will be thankful for your creativity!

The Macy's Thanksgiving Day Parade is famous for its large balloons shaped like popular characters.

TURKEY DAY
Did you know that the wild turkey almost became the national bird of the United States? Benjamin Franklin, one of the nation's founders, proposed the turkey as the national symbol. But it lost to the bald eagle!

Thanksgiving Who's Who

Pilgrims and Native Americans shared a huge feast at the first Thanksgiving celebration.

When you think of Thanksgiving, you may think of two groups of people—Pilgrims and **Native** Americans. That is because the holiday has its roots in the relationship between these groups.

In the 1600s, the Church of England firmly controlled how people were allowed to practice religion in England.

However, many people disagreed with the church. One group of people, called the Separatists, wanted to be able to worship God in their own way. They moved to Holland to escape the church's rules. Soon after, they decided to venture across the Atlantic Ocean. By setting up a **colony** in North America, the Separatists could start new lives away from the church's influence. We call these settlers Pilgrims because a pilgrim is someone who travels a long way, often for religious reasons.

The Pilgrims were not the first people in North America. Many native people had already been there for thousands of years. The Wampanoags were one of the many native groups in North America. They lived in the area that is now eastern Massachusetts, where they survived by hunting, gathering, fishing, and farming the land.

The Pilgrims settled at a place now called Plymouth, Massachusetts, in late 1620. There, they experienced a harsh first winter. Many died from illness and lack of food. In the spring, they met the Wampanoags. The Pilgrims and Native Americans signed a **treaty** agreeing not to fight or steal from each other. The Native Americans taught the Pilgrims how to farm the land. After the summer, the Pilgrims had **abundant** crops. William Bradford, the governor of the colony, declared that the Pilgrims should set aside a day to be thankful and celebrate.

A Three-Day Celebration

A juicy roast turkey is the main course at most modern Thanksgiving celebrations.

What do you eat for Thanksgiving? Some traditional foods include turkey, stuffing, mashed potatoes, and cranberry sauce. Many people also serve pumpkin pie, apple pie, and corn bread on Thanksgiving. Your family might have other favorites, too. But not all of these foods were eaten at the original **harvest** celebration held by the Pilgrims and the Wampanoags. Based on a letter written at the time, historians know the guests ate "fowl," which refers to wild birds. This may have meant duck and geese. Historians also know that the Wampanoags brought venison—deer meat. Other foods, such as corn, beans, and squash (including pumpkin), were a common part of the colonial diet.

Historians also know that the guests played games. We don't know exactly what they did. But we do know that they celebrated and feasted for three days. There were about 90 Wampanoag men and about 50 colonists at the harvest festival. How many people come to your Thanksgiving dinner?

Lots of food, lots of guests, and lots of fun. Does that sound like the way you celebrate Thanksgiving today?

Pumpkin pie is often topped with whipped cream for a tasty Thanksgiving dessert.

A NATIONAL HOLIDAY

Thanksgiving was not observed annually after this first celebration in colonial times. People declared days of thanks at different times of the year when they had reason to celebrate something. It wasn't until 1863 that President Abraham Lincoln declared Thanksgiving a national holiday to be held on the fourth Thursday of November every year.

Basic Tools

You'll need a variety of tools and supplies to create these fun Thanksgiving crafts. Always keep a pencil and scrap paper handy to jot down ideas or sketch out a plan for a project. You often need scissors, tape, glue, and a ruler, too. Here are other supplies you might need:

Papers

Cardboard is a stiff paper good for making **templates**. Cardstock paper is thick and stronger than regular paper. The brown paper from grocery bags is thin and easy to fold.

Markers

Permanent markers work well on paper, wood, and cardboard. Special fabric markers are better for drawing on canvas and other fabrics.

Painting Tools

You will need paintbrushes of various sizes, a container of water, and a paper towel. You can use a paper plate as a **palette** for holding and mixing paint. Acrylic paint is easy to wash off your hands and comes in many colors. (*See page 12 for painting tips.*)

Sewing Tools

Canvas is a thick woven fabric. Felt is softer. You can buy them both by the yard (meter). Felt also comes in smaller craft sheets. Both are easy to cut and draw on. These fabrics hold together well when gluing or sewing.

To sew pieces of fabric together, you will need a needle and thread, fabric scissors, and straight pins to hold layers of fabric in place. (*See pages 12–13 for sewing tips.*)

Other Materials

For some projects in this book, you may also need:

- Wooden clothespins and skewers
- Jute (a type of twine made from plant fibers)
- Pinecones
- Cornhusks
- Birdseed and peanut butter
- Small white beans, dried cranberries, and popcorn

THANKSGIVING SYMBOLS
As you are decorating for the holidays, you may want to use some of these common Thanksgiving symbols in your creations:
- cornucopias
- turkeys
- autumn leaves
- pumpkins
- cranberries, corn, beans, and wheat
- cornstalks
- Pilgrim hats

Popular colors for the holiday include brown, orange, and yellow.

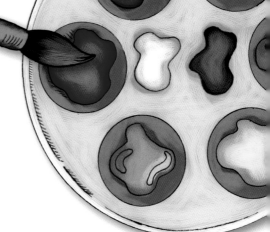

Painting and Sewing Tips

Painting

Here are a few tips to keep in mind when you paint:

- Keep yourself and your workspace clean. Cover the area with newspapers. Wear a smock or apron.
- Squeeze the amount of paint you think you'll need onto a paper plate. This will be your palette. You can use the brush and palette to mix colors together.
- Rinse your brush well in a container of water before dipping it into a new color of paint. Dry it with a paper towel.
- When you are done with your project, toss out the paper plate palette. Clean your brush with warm soapy water, and let it dry before you put it away.

Sewing

With just a few simple stitches, you can sew like a pro! Here are some tips:

Threading a needle: Make sure you have good lighting. Hold the needle steady, and poke the thread through the eye of the needle. You may have to try a few times to get it right! Pull the thread through the eye until the two ends meet. Then tie them in a knot. That way you won't have to worry about the thread slipping out of the needle.

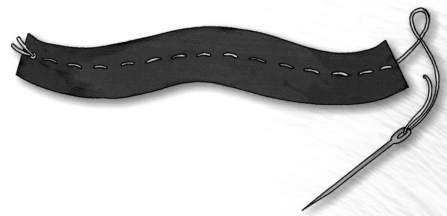

Running stitch: This is a basic in-and-out stitch. Poke the needle down into the fabric, and pull it until it stops at the knot. Then poke the needle up through the fabric, and pull it all the way through. Repeat until you reach the end. Try to keep your stitches straight and even.

Blanket stitch: This stitch makes a decorative edge. To start, poke the needle into the fabric about ¼ inch (6 millimeters) from the edge. Then poke it back up through the fabric at the edge.

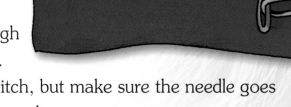

Repeat on the next stitch, but make sure the needle goes through the loop of thread you create.

Securing the end: When you reach the end of the fabric, poke the needle in and out again very close together, but don't pull it all the way through. Instead, poke the needle through the loop made by the thread. Then pull it all the way through. Repeat this step to make a double knot. Trim off the extra thread with fabric scissors.

Stuffed Turkey Puppet

Help this stuffed turkey puppet run
away before someone eats him for dinner!

Materials
- 2 rounded wooden clothespins
- White paint, paintbrush, and palette
- About ½ yard (45 centimeters) of brown felt (or 4 felt sheets)
- Ruler
- Fabric scissors
- Permanent marker
- Straight pins
- Needle and thread
- Felt scraps or craft stuffing

Steps
1. Paint the rounded ends of the clothespins. Set them aside to dry.
2. Cut out two 5- by 6-inch (13 by 15 cm) pieces of felt. Use the marker to draw a large teardrop shape on one of the

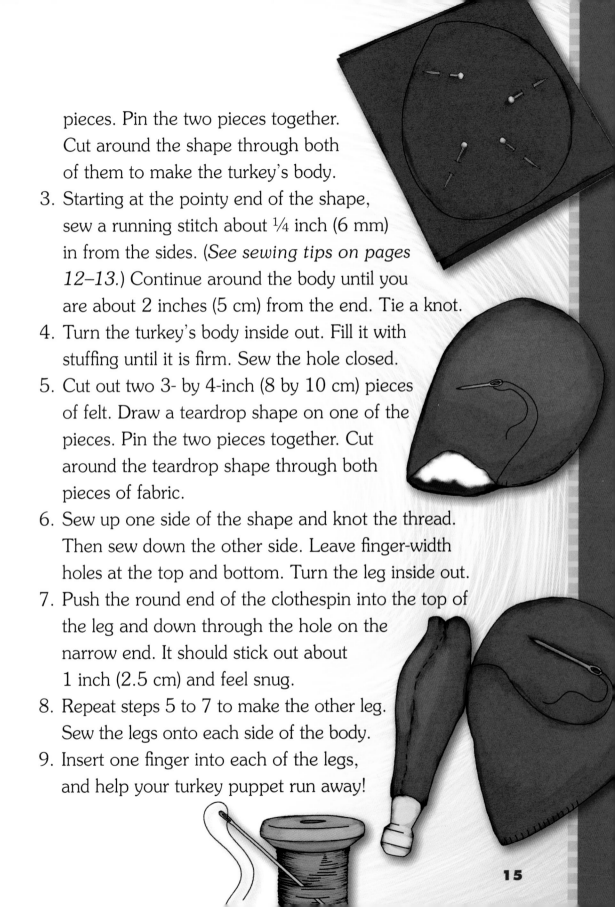

pieces. Pin the two pieces together. Cut around the shape through both of them to make the turkey's body.

3. Starting at the pointy end of the shape, sew a running stitch about ¼ inch (6 mm) in from the sides. (*See sewing tips on pages 12–13.*) Continue around the body until you are about 2 inches (5 cm) from the end. Tie a knot.

4. Turn the turkey's body inside out. Fill it with stuffing until it is firm. Sew the hole closed.

5. Cut out two 3- by 4-inch (8 by 10 cm) pieces of felt. Draw a teardrop shape on one of the pieces. Pin the two pieces together. Cut around the teardrop shape through both pieces of fabric.

6. Sew up one side of the shape and knot the thread. Then sew down the other side. Leave finger-width holes at the top and bottom. Turn the leg inside out.

7. Push the round end of the clothespin into the top of the leg and down through the hole on the narrow end. It should stick out about 1 inch (2.5 cm) and feel snug.

8. Repeat steps 5 to 7 to make the other leg. Sew the legs onto each side of the body.

9. Insert one finger into each of the legs, and help your turkey puppet run away!

Cornucopia

A cornucopia is a popular decoration on Thanksgiving. This "horn of plenty" symbolizes the abundance of a good crop. A cornucopia is usually made from a woven basket. But you can make your own using grocery bags!

Materials
- 3 brown paper grocery bags
- Scissors
- Ruler
- Masking tape
- White glue

Steps
1. Cut a brown paper bag down one side. Then cut off the bottom and unfold it so you have a large sheet of paper. Repeat this step with the other two bags.
2. Roll one of the sheets of brown paper into a cone shape. Tape it closed with masking tape. Trim the edges so the hole in the top is an even circle.
3. Cut a long 3-inch (8 cm) wide strip from one of the bags. Set it aside. Cut the rest of the bags into long strips that are 1 inch (2.5 cm) wide. Fold each of these strips in half.

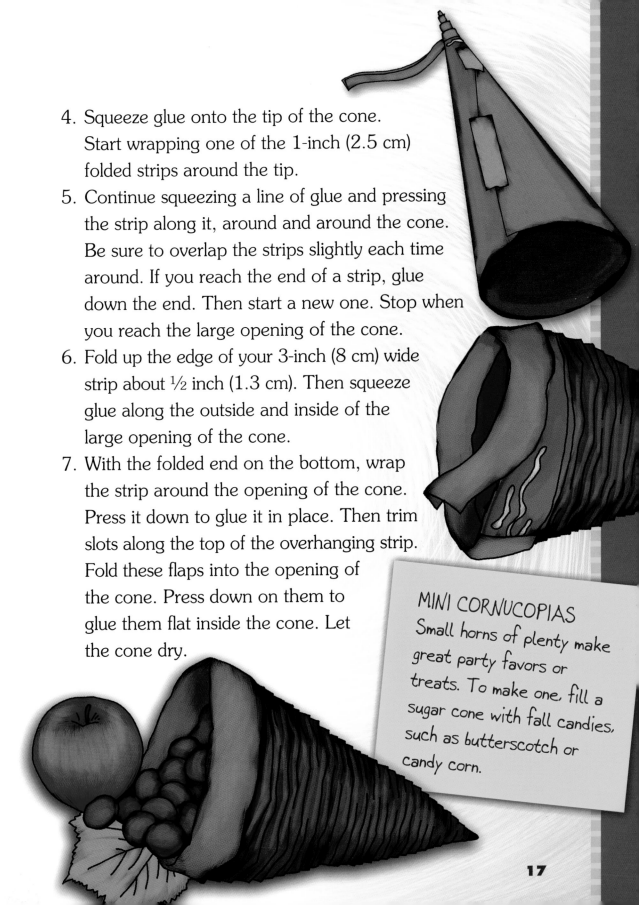

4. Squeeze glue onto the tip of the cone. Start wrapping one of the 1-inch (2.5 cm) folded strips around the tip.

5. Continue squeezing a line of glue and pressing the strip along it, around and around the cone. Be sure to overlap the strips slightly each time around. If you reach the end of a strip, glue down the end. Then start a new one. Stop when you reach the large opening of the cone.

6. Fold up the edge of your 3-inch (8 cm) wide strip about ½ inch (1.3 cm). Then squeeze glue along the outside and inside of the large opening of the cone.

7. With the folded end on the bottom, wrap the strip around the opening of the cone. Press it down to glue it in place. Then trim slots along the top of the overhanging strip. Fold these flaps into the opening of the cone. Press down on them to glue them flat inside the cone. Let the cone dry.

MINI CORNUCOPIAS
Small horns of plenty make great party favors or treats. To make one, fill a sugar cone with fall candies, such as butterscotch or candy corn.

Thank You Banner

Ask your guests to make flags for the banner. Then display everyone's creations.

Materials

- Cardboard, pencil, ruler, scissors (for template)
- ½ yard (45 cm) canvas fabric in a light color, such as tan or yellow
- Fabric scissors
- 2 felt sheets in a darker color, such as brown or orange
- Permanent marker
- Straight pins
- Needle and thread (or white glue)
- 3 yards (2.7 meters) jute
- Fabric markers

10 inches

4 inches

Steps

1. Cut a piece of cardboard to be about 4 inches (10 cm) wide and 10 inches (25 cm) high. Trace it onto the canvas 12 times. Cut out the rectangles.
2. Cut the template in half so that it measures 4 by 5 inches (10 by 13 cm). Trace this shape onto the felt six times. Cut out these rectangles.

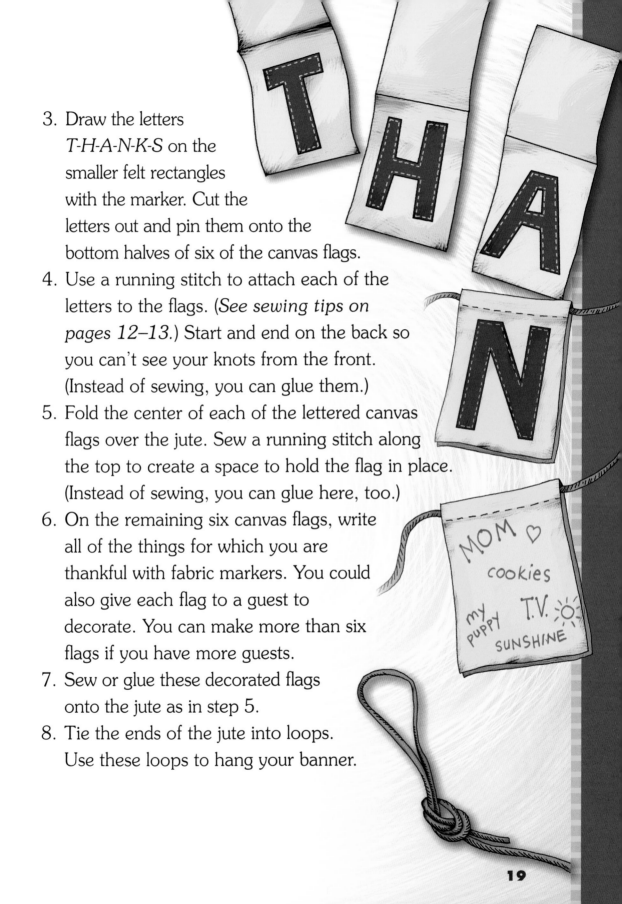

3. Draw the letters *T-H-A-N-K-S* on the smaller felt rectangles with the marker. Cut the letters out and pin them onto the bottom halves of six of the canvas flags.

4. Use a running stitch to attach each of the letters to the flags. (*See sewing tips on pages 12–13.*) Start and end on the back so you can't see your knots from the front. (Instead of sewing, you can glue them.)

5. Fold the center of each of the lettered canvas flags over the jute. Sew a running stitch along the top to create a space to hold the flag in place. (Instead of sewing, you can glue here, too.)

6. On the remaining six canvas flags, write all of the things for which you are thankful with fabric markers. You could also give each flag to a guest to decorate. You can make more than six flags if you have more guests.

7. Sew or glue these decorated flags onto the jute as in step 5.

8. Tie the ends of the jute into loops. Use these loops to hang your banner.

Pilgrim Place Cards

Make place cards for each of your Thanksgiving guests. These Pilgrims will greet them when they sit down for their meal.

Materials

- Pencil and paper
- Rounded wooden clothespins (two for each place card)
- Acrylic paints (in a variety of colors), paintbrush, palette
- Black permanent marker
- Orange and white felt
- Scissors
- White glue
- Cardstock paper
- Ruler

Steps

1. Sketch out ideas for how you want your Pilgrims to look. Once you have decided on a look, draw the designs onto your clothespins lightly in pencil.
2. Squeeze the paints you need onto your palette. Use a brush to paint the large areas of color on the clothespins, such as the Pilgrims' shirts and pants. Rinse your brush well

anytime you switch colors. Let the paint dry before continuing.

3. Next, paint on details such as sleeves and hair. If you want a Pilgrim to wear a hat, paint the top of its head. You will make the rest of the hat out of felt later.

4. Use a permanent marker to add small details, such as eyes, legs, and shoes.

5. To make a hat with a brim, cut out a small circle of orange felt. Cut an even smaller circle in the center. Test to see if it will fit on your Pilgrim's head. Trim it if needed. Squeeze a line of glue around the Pilgrim's head. Place the brim on its head.

6. You can also make a hood and collar. Cut out a small rectangle (for the hood) and two small triangles (for the collar). Test it on the Pilgrim and trim it to the right size. Squeeze glue on the top of its head and hold the hood in place until it sticks. Glue the triangles at the neckline.

7. Cut a piece of cardstock that is 4 inches (10 cm) wide by 2 inches (5 cm) high. Write the name of your guest in the center of the card.

8. Stand up the place card by placing it between your Pilgrims.

COLONIAL DRESS
In colonial times, men wore tops called doublets and pants called breeches. Women wore a waistcoat on top and petticoats under their skirts. They both wore long socks called stockings.

Feast for the Birds

Share the spirit of Thanksgiving with birds by decorating a tree with pinecone feeders and popcorn perches.

Materials for a Pinecone Feeder

- Pinecones
- Jute
- Scissors
- Peanut butter
- Spreading knife
- Birdseed
- Pan with high sides

Steps

1. Take a walk outdoors and collect some pinecones. Tie a loop of jute on the stem end of each pinecone.
2. Spread a few tablespoons of peanut butter onto each pinecone. Try to get the peanut butter into most of the openings.
3. Pour some birdseed into a pan with high sides so it doesn't spill. Roll the peanut butter pinecones in the birdseed. The seeds will stick to the peanut butter.
4. Hang your feeders on branches outside.

Materials for a Popcorn Perch

- Needle and thread
- Ruler
- Scissors
- Wooden skewer
- Dried cranberries
- Popcorn
- Jute

Steps

1. Thread a needle, and pull the thread through about 18 inches (46 cm). Cut the thread, and knot the ends of the strands together. Tie the end of the thread to the end of the wooden skewer.
2. Poke the needle into a dried cranberry, and string it onto your thread. Push it all the way to the end. Next, string on a piece of popcorn. Continue **alternating** between cranberries and popcorn until the strand measures about 12 inches (30 cm).
3. Wind the strand of popcorn and cranberries around the skewer. Tie the thread to the other end of the skewer.
4. Cut a piece of jute that is about 24 inches (60 cm) long. Tie the ends of the jute to the ends of the skewer.
5. Use the jute to hang the skewer on a branch outside. Birds will be able to perch while they eat.

Cornhusk Doll

Wampanoag children made dolls out of natural items, such as cornhusks. If your family is serving fresh corn at your Thanksgiving feast, save the husks. You can make them into dolls like children did long ago.

Materials

- Cornhusks from 2 to 3 ears of corn
- Scissors
- 1 small rubber band
- Jute

Steps

1. Trim the pointy ends from the tops of the husks. Tear some of the husks into 1-inch (2.5 cm) wide strips.
2. Gather six of these strips together at the narrow ends. Secure this bundle about 1 inch (2.5 cm) down from the top very tightly with a rubber band.
3. Fold the husks down over the rubber band so the rubber band is no longer visible. Cut a short length of jute and tie it tightly under the rubber band. This will be your doll's head.

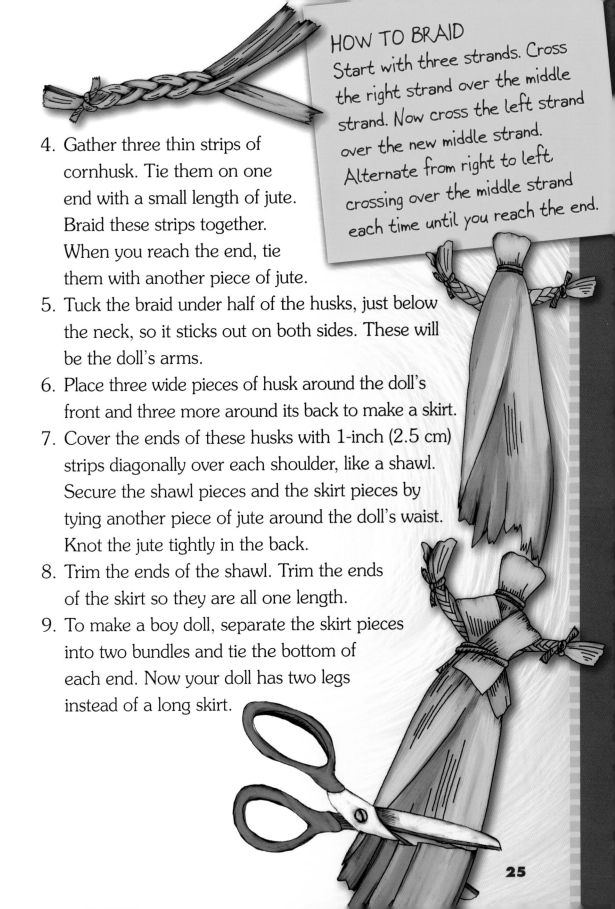

Start with three strands. Cross the right strand over the middle strand. Now cross the left strand over the new middle strand. Alternate from right to left, crossing over the middle strand each time until you reach the end.

4. Gather three thin strips of cornhusk. Tie them on one end with a small length of jute. Braid these strips together. When you reach the end, tie them with another piece of jute.

5. Tuck the braid under half of the husks, just below the neck, so it sticks out on both sides. These will be the doll's arms.

6. Place three wide pieces of husk around the doll's front and three more around its back to make a skirt.

7. Cover the ends of these husks with 1-inch (2.5 cm) strips diagonally over each shoulder, like a shawl. Secure the shawl pieces and the skirt pieces by tying another piece of jute around the doll's waist. Knot the jute tightly in the back.

8. Trim the ends of the shawl. Trim the ends of the skirt so they are all one length.

9. To make a boy doll, separate the skirt pieces into two bundles and tie the bottom of each end. Now your doll has two legs instead of a long skirt.

Arrowhead Beanbag Toss

Historians know that the Pilgrims and Wampanoags played games as part of the Thanksgiving festivities. These games may have included archery and rifle contests. You and a friend can have a competition of your own with beanbags shaped like arrowheads.

Materials

- Cardboard, pencil, ruler, scissors (for template)
- Permanent marker
- 2 brown felt sheets (or another color of your choice)
- 2 gray felt sheets (or another color of your choice)
- Straight pins
- Fabric scissors
- Needle and thread
- 1 red felt sheet (or another color of your choice)
- 1 white felt sheet (or another color of your choice)
- 1½ cups small dry white beans
- White glue

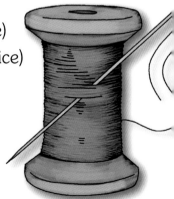

Steps

1. Draw an arrowhead shape about 4 inches (10 cm) wide and 5 inches (13 cm) high on a piece of cardboard. Cut it out with scissors. This will be your template.
2. Trace your template onto one sheet of the brown felt four times with the marker. Then pin the two brown sheets of felt together. Use the fabric scissors to cut out the arrowheads through both layers of felt, so that you have four pinned pairs.
3. Repeat step 2 with the gray felt.
4. For each arrowhead, sew a running stitch from the bottom corner, around the top of the arrowhead, and down the other side. (*See sewing tips on pages 12–13.*) Knot the end. Leave the bottom open. Repeat with the other seven arrowheads. Turn them all inside out through the bottom hole.
5. Fill each of the arrowheads with about 3 tablespoons of beans.
6. Use a blanket stitch to seal the bottom of each arrowhead. (*See sewing tips on pages 12–13.*)

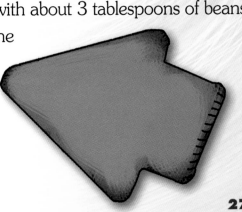

7. To make a target, pin the red and white felt sheets together. Draw a large circle shape on the red felt. Cut out both sheets so that you have two large circles. Set the white circle aside.

8. Draw two smaller circles on the red circle. Cut out the middle ring so that you are left with a red circle for the center and a round frame around the outside.

9. Glue the red ring and the small red circle onto the large white felt circle.

10. Now you're ready for a game of toss!

HOW TO PLAY

Play this fun game with a partner. One player can take the gray arrowheads, and the other can take the brown. Place the target about 5 feet (1.5 m) away on the floor. The game works best on carpet. If your floor is too smooth, the target might slide around. Take turns tossing your beanbags at the target. See who can get his or her beanbags closest to the center!

Past and Present

Life was not easy for the Pilgrims. These early colonists moved to an unfamiliar land. They had to make their own clothes and grow their own food. They had to build their own homes. They had to work together as a community so that everyone would have what they needed to survive.

We can imagine what the Pilgrims might have been feeling during their three-day Thanksgiving celebration. Perhaps they were grateful for the rain that watered the crops and the sun that helped them grow. Maybe they were thankful that the fields provided enough food to last the winter. Perhaps they thanked the Wampanoags for their help in making America their new home.

This Thanksgiving, think about the past year of your life. Celebrate the things you are grateful for, just as the Pilgrims did many years ago, with a feast, fun, family, and friends.

What are you thankful for?

Glossary

abundant (uh-BUHN-duhnt) widely available in great amounts

alternating (AWL-tur-nay-ting) going back and forth between two things

annually (AN-yoo-uh-lee) happening once every year

colony (KAHL-uh-nee) an area that has been settled by people from another country and is controlled by that country

harvest (HAHR-vust) the crops gathered at the end of the growing season

native (NAY-tiv) born in a particular country or place

palette (PAL-ut) a flat board that is used for mixing paints

templates (TEM-plits) stiff patterns used to make the same shapes in other materials

traditions (truh-DISH-uhnz) customs, ideas, or beliefs that are handed down from one generation to the next

treaty (TREE-tee) a formal agreement between two or more groups

For More Information

Books

Cunningham, Kevin, and Peter Benoit. *The Wampanoag*. New York: Children's Press, 2011.

Nelson, Robin. *Thanksgiving*. Minneapolis, MN: Lerner, 2010.

Rooney, Ronnie. *Thanksgiving Recipes*. Mankato, MN: Picture Window Books, 2011.

Waxman, Laura Hamilton. *Why Did the Pilgrims Come to the New World? And Other Questions about the Plymouth Colony*. Minneapolis: Lerner, 2011.

Web Sites

History of the Holidays

www.history.com/topics/thanksgiving

Watch videos and read about the history of Thanksgiving.

National Geographic: Wild Turkey

http://animals.nationalgeographic.com/animals/birds/wild-turkey

Find out more about this feathered symbol of the holiday.

Plimoth Plantation

www.plimoth.org/learn/just-kids

Learn all about the Pilgrims, the Wampanoags, and life in colonial times.

Index

About the Author

Dana Meachen Rau is the author of more than 300 books for children on many topics, including science, history, cooking, and crafts. She creates, experiments, researches, and writes from her home office in Burlington, Connecticut.